HOW TO BEAT THE SOCIAL WORKER

AN INSIDE SCOOP

Surviving Children Services Intervention-UK

Copyright

HOW TO BEAT THE SOCIAL WORKER: AN INSIDE SCOOP

Published by
The Full Picture Publishing
Oxford, United Kingdom
www.thefullpicturepublishing.com

A catalogue record for this book is available at the British Library.

Contents

ABOUT THE AUTHOR

James Maynard qualified as a social worker with an M.A. in Social Work in 2012. In his thirteen years in the profession, he has worked in Children's Services in different Local Authorities across the country. He has amassed plenty of experience in frontline social work in Child in Need and Child in Care teams up to management level, facilitating risk management and safeguarding processes in complex family dynamics, which included in-depth court work. He also oversees the training of social work students as a practice educator.

INTRODUCTION

So, you have received a call from the social worker and they want to come out to see you–'have a chat', they may say. You are hit with a flurry of emotions–hope, anxiety, dread, maybe indignation, sometimes anger, shock, disbelief. This is what it will feel like for most people; for a minority, however, it will be a mix of opposite emotions–relief, hope, vindication, joy. This is because the social worker, like the police, is a very useful tool but one that is very much a double-edged sword, and like the police, they mostly appear when something has gone wrong–this time in the family. The only question is–are they coming out at parents' request or that of the general public?

Over the last decade, since I started my career in Social Work, I have encountered so many varied scenarios and situations that families are stuck in as they try to negotiate and find their way through the maze of social work processes. I have noticed a profound but understandable lack of knowledge in parents and wider family members about their rights, those of the child, how the social worker processes the information they gather, what processes they follow, and how this ultimately leads to the final outcome, which could range from a 'No Further Action' to 'Adoption'.

This book has been written to help with this problem. It is written to lay bare the meaning behind the actions of the social worker and to help parents and families predict and prepare for the next step on their journey with social services. It will provide a clear explanation of how the social worker will approach each case depending on the presenting concerns and how you, the parent or extended family, can respond appropriately.

Although this book appears to be very much a cheat guide to interacting with the social worker, the points and tips that it gives can only really be put into effect by parents and families who have the capacity to commit to the welfare of their children. However, as I have seen so very often, sometimes, this capacity, whilst present, is not demonstrated in the right way due to a lack of knowledge of the social work process.

As should be already obvious, this book deals only with child safeguarding and, therefore, Children's Social Services intervention. As should also be already obvious, I have set out to write this book in very plain and easy-to-read language, and I will be breaking down very often-used social work terminology in very simple terms so that the next time you encounter these terms, you know exactly what they mean. I will also be concise in the delivery of the message in this book.

The structure of this book is laid out in steps that move from the diagnosis to the solution and everything in between. So, I will first go through the most common difficulties and scenarios that lead to family breakdown and the involvement of social services, and how this often plays out. Then I will paint the picture of how the social worker will routinely work with the family, and how your response as a parent or family member can lead to outcomes that you want or outcomes that you dread.

I will walk you through how the Local Authority (though each L.A. will have different processes), in general, will take a case through escalation and risk management until they instigate care proceedings against you, the parent. Finally, this book will help you understand how to understand and engage in the court process strictly and only from a perspective of social care, what to expect at the end of this process, and how the worst-case scenarios are not necessarily the end.

WHO IS THE SOCIAL WORKER

There are a lot of misconceptions out there about the work that social workers do. Most people have narrowed it down quite negatively and stereotypically to people who take children away from their parents. Others, usually professionals, have this idea, whether implicitly or explicitly expressed, that social workers are some sort of community worker or child behaviour specialist–in other words, a supernanny. I have had parents and family carers calling up and expecting a social worker to come over and 'fix' a child having a tantrum or 'kicking off' in the home. In these circumstances, I have often wondered what the parent/family carer expects the social worker will achieve that they cannot, considering they know this child, their characteristics, triggers, history, likes, and dislikes a lot more than the social worker does. I have had very frustrated parents struggling to cope with a child who has very difficult behaviours–usually underlined by some neurological condition–who request respite from social services, which is not something they would provide that readily, as it flirts with the idea of getting the child into the care system.

I have taken calls from schools reporting every little misdemeanour of a child open to services, very much like they are expecting the social worker to do something to 'change' the child. I have also had police officers complain that they cannot keep going after missing children, as it ties them down and "they are not social workers". Finally, I have seen community justice activists tag the work that they do as social work.

I have also been requested quite ignorantly and arrogantly by a police officer to come do 'my job' and support the police by using my skills as a social worker to 'talk a child down' who was exhibiting very difficult behaviours.

These misconceptions exist because the term 'social work' is quite a generic one and can be interpreted quite loosely to mean almost anything to do with working with people and the public. However, Social Work is a registered profession with a very defined designation, and while any social worker may, in particular cases, play the role of a community activist, a supernanny, a helper, or a child whisperer, this is not the role they are employed or trained to play.

To put it simply, the child social worker is the principal co-ordinator of the services that a child needs to either have their developmental needs met or to be kept safe from harm. They are tasked to assess and identify these needs, or what harm a child is suffering or could suffer from the care they are receiving from parents, family, or other carers. They are also tasked to take measures to address this harm or meet these needs. Most importantly, in carrying out their role, they represent the Local Authority and work with the backing of legislation. In effect, they are like the child and family police.

To put this into a simpler context, the social worker is not trained to 'parent' the child on the parents' behalf or to 'fix' their difficult behaviours. Instead, they identify the services that can support parents to parent more effectively, and where, for any reason, parents are unable to do this, they identify ways to keep the child safe–and this is where the removal of the child can occur. So, in other words, the social worker can never bring about a quick fix to any parenting or child behavioural issues. However, without their input, there is not likely to be a long-term and well-structured plan to address the problem. So, the next time you pick up the phone to social services, do have this in mind.

The above definition covers all areas of social worker, although the requirement to use the law to bring about a separation between the client and their family occurs most often within children's social work. However, in principle, social workers working with every category of vulnerable people are bound to assess and identify needs or risk of harm and respond to these using the law.

The most important point I will make on the role of the social worker, however, is one that runs counter to the stereotype of the social worker as someone who 'takes children away' from their families. In contrast, the first duty of the social worker by law is to keep children and families together; this includes the wider family, where this is not possible within the immediate family. Where a social worker is more focused on the risks within the family and less on the support that could be put in place to ensure the children are safer and better cared for, then that is not good social work practice. Of course, sometimes the support needed is not sustainable or fails to address the risks to the child; in such cases, more drastic measures would be employed by social services.

REFERRALS TO SOCIAL SERVICES

Referrals can come from a variety of sources, but the two most common avenues are directly from the public and from the police.

Referrals from the Public

Every Local Authority will have a telephone number or other means by which members of the public can report concerns they have about a child or their parents. When these are received, they are processed usually via an initial assessment by that customer facing team; it is the job of this team to downstream this referral after their assessment, either for lower level of intervention from a Family Support Practitioner (could have a different name in other L. As) or to social care for a social work assessment.

Referrals from the public, on their own, usually present social workers with the weakest body of evidence for the social worker to start an assessment. This is because one point that is not expressed enough is that the social worker has no business in your home and your life without reasonable and evidenced cause. Just like the police cannot arrest without reasonable cause, the social worker has no right to your time and your home without reasonable cause. A referral from the public in itself does not constitute reasonable cause. It is not strong enough. However, in my experience, where a referral from the public progresses to a social work assessment, it is because there would have been a strong history of interventions with the family in question and other professional observations to back up the referral. So, usually, the initial assessment to investigate the referral from the public would be to look for corroborating reports from other professionals or agencies involved with the child, to find evidence of reasonable cause.

Let's consider this example. You have received a phone call or letter from a social worker saying they have received a referral from the police and want to start an assessment to ascertain the safety of the children in the home. You ask what the referral is about, and you are informed that it is one that relates to a historical allegation against you of physical or sexual abuse. However, you are aware that the allegations they speak of were investigated by the police at the time and NFA'd. You also know that this is all the social worker has to go on in requesting this social work assessment. You are well within your rights to refuse them access to your time and your home; they do not have the reasonable cause or evidence to suggest your children are at risk of harm and, therefore, have no right to intrude into your life.

The above example is simply to demonstrate how reasonable cause or the absence of it works, and the absence of reasonable cause usually presents itself in public referrals. The example above is from a police referral, which I will discuss next, but in reality, police referrals, way more often than not, come with evidenced of reasonable cause for social care intervention.

Police Referrals

Police referrals are the other most common source of social services referrals, and these usually occur when the police have had to visit a property in the line of duty and encountered criminal activity taking place there with a child present. That in itself is an unimpeachable body of evidence that gives social services the reasonable cause they need to request an assessment of the child's life within their family. Depending on the risk that the presenting situation poses to the child, which is judged by other factors including the age and understanding of the child, and the presentation of the parents and the home, the case can be treated at a lower or higher level of social services intervention. Suppose the parent or both parents are arrested so that the child has to go to someone else (usually in the wider family) to be cared for; the case will usually be treated under a Child Protection Plan, which is an advanced level of safeguarding that social services employ. More on this later.

If, however, there was another parent who holds parental responsibility for the child and is not implicated in the offence of the first parent, then this case would usually not need to go to a Child Protection Plan. This other parent can exercise their parental responsibility and care for the child safely; of course, there would still be a social work assessment to ensure that this arrangement is safe and to provide support where there are difficulties identified.

Parental Responsibility

It is best at this point to talk about parental responsibility and what powers it gives the parent in interacting with social services and the police in respect of social care. When the police show up at your door, as is with any other scenario, the weight of the power they carry often makes people forget or not realise what rights and powers they also have. The singularly biggest power a parent possesses when dealing with social services or the police in respect of social care is their parental responsibility. Where a parent gets arrested for a crime and is bailed under certain conditions, which may include restrictions on contact with the child, their parental responsibility to care for the child does not cease, but is now opposed by the power of the police to keep the public safe. So, if the said parent were to breach these conditions, they would be committing an offence of breaching bail conditions.

However, where a parent is not arrested by the police but is given certain stipulations as advised by social services, they still retain the right to wield parental responsibility as long as they can address the presenting concerns. I think it is best to give an example here.

Let's assume the police visit a home on a Thursday morning due to reports of domestic violence between parents and find them both intoxicated. The offending parent is arrested and removed from the property, but the police are worried about the alcohol use by the victim's parent. Added to this, the nine-year-old child present in the home reports that her mother is often drunk when she gets home from school. The police seek advice from social services, and they both agree the child should not be left alone at home with the mother until social services can begin a social work assessment the following Monday to fully explore the mother's alcohol use and put together a safety plan. The child goes to stay with a family friend down the road from Thursday until Friday, and then goes off to school.

A social worker arrives at the home on Friday morning to put in place a plan for the weekend–who other adult would come into the home, or where could the child go for the weekend? Mother has had enough and tells the social worker to forget about such a plan. She would take care of her daughter and does not want anyone else in her home. The social worker is worried and calls the police seeking a possible drastic measure of the child being taken out of the home under police protection. The police arrive and meet a sober and clear-thinking mother who restates her position to care for her daughter.

Due to the fact that the presenting concerns (intoxication) no longer exist at that moment in time, there would be clearly no risk of imminent harm to the child, not even a risk of neglect, and that would remove any justification for such a drastic measure. Even if the mother was intoxicated, there would be an assessment of the risk of harm or neglect she poses to the child, considering the child's age, capacity for self-care, and the mother's history before such a drastic measure could be taken. This is just one demonstration of the power of a parent's right to exercise parental authority over a child's welfare.

Some other facts about parental responsibility:

- Mothers acquire P.R. by natural right.
- Fathers generally have to be named on the birth certificate to acquire P.R., or they can get this from the Court.
- A person with P.R. never loses it until and unless the child in question gets adopted, whereupon the P.R. is taken up by the adoptive parent.

Where the Local Authority is granted a Care Order over a child, they share P.R. with parents, but their P.R. stands higher than that of parents in making decisions for the child.

- A family member other than the parents can also acquire P.R. from the court through an order like the Special Guardianship Order.

Until a Care Order is granted, the Local Authority do not have P.R. and no right to make decisions about a child; the social worker must defer to parents for all decisions about the child and must seek their consent to engage with the child for the purposes of an assessment.

However, in respect of the point above, where there is reasonable cause that the child may be suffering significant harm and the social worker is conducting what is called a section 47 investigation, they can see and speak to the child for the purposes of this assessment without consent.

Until the Local Authority acquires P.R. for a child, parents retain the right to care for their child and are under no obligation to work with the social worker or with professionals. However, a failure to do this could count as evidence (where other valid concerns exist) that could be built up to show that the child could be at risk of significant harm and used in legal proceedings against the parent/s.

Finally, a child may be in the care of the Local Authority through an arrangement willingly agreed by parents, which is referred to as a section 20 care arrangement. In such a scenario, the parents still hold full P.R. over the child, and the Local Authority can only make decisions for the child with the consent of the parents.

So, let's say, for example, a child has been signed into a section 20 care arrangement by his father, who has been caring for him. Mother had been denied custody of the child earlier by the court in favour of the father, but now the child is in the care of the Local Authority, her P.R. comes back into play at the same level as the father's. By virtue of the same P.R., the mother requests her son back into her care, which the Local Authority has to comply with unless they identify a reasonable cause to believe this would put the child at risk of harm. An assessment is completed, and this is positive with a recommendation for support to be put in place to support mother care for the boy. The boy is transitioned back to his mother's care, and as to be expected, the mother is nervous about having to play the role of main carer again. Mother keeps calling the social worker to check if her planned decisions would be acceptable; the social worker keeps reminding mother that she has P.R and had the power to make decisions even whilst the child was still in the care of the Local Authority–although these could clash with the Local Authority's care plan and would then require a conversation/negotiation. Mother, certainly, does not need the social worker's approval to make care decisions for the boy now that he is fully in mother's care.

Or take this other example where a child is under the care of an uncle and aunt under a Special Guardianship Order. Due to issues in the care she is being given, this is taken back to court and a Supervision Order is granted for the Local Authority to monitor the care given to the child for a period of six months for those specific issues.

The child is now under a Child in Need Plan, which is being reviewed every 6 weeks. At the end of the six-month period of the Supervision Order, and when it had been demonstrated that these issues had not recurred, uncle and aunt did not wait for the Local Authority to review and wind down the CIN plan; they simply disengaged from social services.

The fact that they had P.R. gave them the right to do this, especially as there is now no (Supervision) order that obliged them to work with social services. Furthermore, they know there are no valid concerns that could be used to build evidence that the child could be at risk of harm from their disengagement.

Family Arrangement

Another area where the power of parental responsibility can be exercised is in the use of family arrangements. When a parent has been judged as not safe to care for a child for any reason and there is no other person with P.R. around, the parent/s can set up a family arrangement with a broader family and friends network. This is where the parent/s propose or agree with the social worker–and very often the police–for the child to go and live with and be cared for by a member of the wider family or a friend.

This choice should and usually is respected by social services and the police, and is seen as an arrangement that has been made by the person with P.R. Sometimes, a social worker may seek to run a police check on the family/friend carer that the parent/s have proposed. This is unnecessary as it is a family arrangement and not one by social services. Parent/s have P.R. and have the right to decide who can care for their child.

If, however, social services insist on a police check, maybe because they cannot trust your choice as a parent, probably due to the presenting concerns, as in the case of chronic neglect or drug use, then they are now making the arrangement a formal one, put together by social services. Where this happens, and your proposed family/friend carer's police check comes back with little or no concerns or something not strong enough to disqualify them, then your family/friend carers will be entitled to an allowance from social services to care for your child. They will be so entitled because by running that police check, social services have sanctioned those carers as people they have chosen and approved, and the arrangement, as one they are accountable for.

When are parent/s and families trusted to make a safe family arrangement?

Sometimes, parent/s and family may not be trusted by social services to be able to make good choices when it comes to a family/friend caring arrangement. In this case, social services may choose to run a police check on the proposed family/friend carers, which then makes the arrangement one set up by social services.

A parent/s or family will generally be trusted to be able to make safe decisions on family/friend carers where the case is one where the child is not suffering (significant) neglect, which is a marker that the parents/family understand what a child needs to be safe. Where there is a single or limited risk issue, but the general care of the child is good and not neglectful, we can trust the family to understand what good care looks like.

For instance, a parent with alcohol misuse, mental health, or domestic violence concerns–with a safe social services history, a good, clean home, a child going to school daily, no issues with schoolwork, well fed, good emotional attention from parents, etc. We can trust such a parent understands what good care looks like, and they can make a safe decision on who can care for their child.

On the other hand, where there is a poor social services history or significant neglect, regardless of the causes, the parent/s' understanding of the rounded safe care a child needs cannot be easily trusted, and any suggestions they make of a carer may be police checked.

Remember, Parent/s have the right to make these family arrangements, and when it is parent/s doing so, there would automatically be consent from the parent/s and they would come up with the suggestion of a family carer themselves.

When, on the other hand, it is social services making the arrangement, the choice would be one that either overrides or is against the consent of the parents, or it would be when social services seek to and run a police check on your proposed family carer.

However, a family arrangement (by definition, one arranged by parents) is only ever a short-term measure.

If the difficulty with parent/s persists and the child cannot return home for some time, then the family carer will need to be assessed for their authority to care for the child to be formalised. When this happens, there will be a DBS (Disclosure and Barring Service) check or, at the very least, a police check on them.

Referrals from Agencies/Professionals

Every other referral to social services will come from this source–every agency, body, or professional working with the child, for example, school, GP, nursery, any extra-curricular club, etc. These referrals can often stand on their own in terms of the weight of evidence they carry. This is because these professionals usually have first-hand and close-up observation of the child. So, if the nursery is reporting that the child comes in often unkempt, hungry, and looking tired, that would be enough reason for a social worker or maybe a family support practitioner to contact you to understand the child's care at home better.

If any of these referrals don't come with a strong evidence base, then, as with any other referral, this evidence base is built up or looked for in the initial assessment by the team looking at the general picture for the child. To do this, the assessment team will try to see what the records show about any other reports, historical or otherwise, that have come in for the child from other agencies, bodies, or professionals.

DEALING WITH INTERVENTION DUE TO MENTAL HEALTH

Poor mental health is one of the three principal issues, also known as the Toxic Trio, that can adversely impact a family and make it difficult for the unit to function healthily; the other two are 'domestic violence' and 'substance misuse', both dealt with in later chapters. Rarely is any of these three present in isolation; where there is one to the extent that social services intervention is necessary, there usually is another or both of the other ones. For the purposes of these chapters, I will deal with each in isolation, so it is clear what combination of strategies you, as a parent, can employ when dealing with intervention for a combination of the trio.

Once the parents' capacity to care adequately is compromised by poor mental health, everything else can so easily fall apart. All the same, there are lots of families' social services that support keeping the children safely cared for at home, where the poor mental health of at least one parent is a live issue. It all comes down to what insight the parent in question has about their own limitations and certain decisions they are able to make at the right time.

Like with everything else, about the biggest tool a parent can have in the task of having the children remain in the family, in the case of poor mental health, is the family/friends' network. An insightful parent who is aware of the potential difficulties their mental health could pose to their ability to parent safely and can gauge how this capacity deteriorates in line with how they are feeling may have already made prior arrangements with the family/friend's network on what support they can give. The main skill here for the parent is a capacity for truthful insight into the state of their mental health, how secure it is, its impact on their everyday functioning, and how to judge when their mental health is deteriorating. With this skill firmly in place, the trick then is to involve the family network via a family arrangement to step into the care role of the parent at the required opportunity. Where this is done with seamless planning, not only would there be no need for social services involvement in the first place, but the children would be no wiser about the situation of the parent, depending on their age.

Take, for example, a single parent with vast levels of anxiety who has been dealing with a lot of stress about work, relationships, and the child's education. One Friday evening, they begin to notice their anxiety levels rising; thoughts swirling in their head uncontrollably; heart racing, head swimming, they feel sick. They pick up the phone, but the first person they call is their mother, as they had prearranged. The parent describes their situation, and the grandmother understands immediately what she needs to do. She hops over, picks up the five-year-old in the home, and both the parent and grandparent give the boy a story that the parent has a headache and needs rest. By this time, the parent has also called the mental health crisis team in their locality. The team visits after the grandmother has left with the child, and the parent is admitted into the hospital, where they spend the weekend. By Tuesday evening, the parent has achieved a state of equilibrium and can pick up the child from school. Both their lives continue as normal.

In contrast, in similar circumstances, instead of the parents calling a grandparent or someone else in the family network, they call social services and request that the child be taken from them, as they are in the midst of an episode and cannot care for the child. The social worker comes and arranges for the child to go to a member of the family network. However, due to more assessments of the parents' state and uncertainty on how long it would take the parents to achieve consistency in equilibrium and seeking to achieve stability for the child, care proceedings are initiated, and the child is made a kinship foster carer for the child. Despite the child still being in the family, the parent now has no right to care for him, not without going back to the court to discharge the care order, which is another hill to climb.

As seen above, the big difference between both scenarios lies in the family being able to make this arrangement and implement it before professionals get involved. Of course, in many cases, one would not be able to control and plan for the impact of one's poor mental health. A parent can spiral into a dark place of depression or other mental states quite quickly, and professionals may get involved sooner than they would have preferred. In those cases, it is imperative that the parent and family network show a very united front before the social worker; ideally, they should have already worked out a solid plan of care for the child where the family network actively supports the parent caring for the child in the parent's own home. Alternatively, the parent and family network should all express an agreement with the social worker to prioritise the welfare of the child. The most important voice here is that of the parent.

The social worker will want to know that the parent is happy and committed to not removing the child from the care of the family network or that the family network will not pull away from the plan of care until the parent is assessed as having achieved a certain level of stability by a mental health practitioner. There could be a wellness plan laid out by the MH practitioner that the parent can show they are working on, medication they are taking, lifestyle changes they are making, etc. As long as this commitment is expressed to the social worker and there is some evidence to show that the parent is prepared or keeping to this commitment, the family arrangement is very likely to be respected, and social services will back away.

Advocates

A parent with a mental health difficulty will very likely be a vulnerable person in their own right, and for them to have to deal with social workers and other professionals on their own can be very daunting and constitutes a strong imbalance of power. Where the parent can get another family member to support them and act as an advocate in meetings, that would be appropriate. However, the parent has the right to request that the Local Authority provide them with a professional advocate for all their meetings. This is a duty on the Local Authority if they are to show that their engagement with the parent has been fair, balanced, and the parent has had the right support–emotionally and cognitively–to take part in meetings with professionals.

If you are a parent with a mental health difficulty and facing intervention by social services, it is always a welcome idea to request the support of a professional advocate. These people have been trained to understand your needs and make sure they support you accordingly in meetings; these can range from making sure you understand what is being said in meetings, helping you understand the processes, advocating for breaks so you have more time to deal with the emotional impact of the meeting–the list is inexhaustive. Of course, you may feel much more comfortable with a family member, but requesting a professional advocate and seeing what support they can offer, in addition, can only be a good thing.

DEALING WITH INTERVENTION DUE TO DOMESTIC VIOLENCE

Since we are relational in nature and need others to survive, it is no surprise that domestic violence in families is the most common of these three major issues and accounts for the highest incidence of social services intervention. Domestic violence is almost always triggered or exacerbated by one or both of the other two: substance misuse and poor mental health.

The intervention for domestic violence is never clear-cut, as it depends a lot on the severity of the confrontation, the age of the child, and their level of development to gauge the level of risk. Generally, the younger the child is and the more physical the altercation, the higher the chances that intervention will be escalated to more advanced risk management processes.

In the case of domestic violence, you, the parent, have to be able to admit the truth to yourself about your situation and that of your partner–the truth being the underlying reason behind your frequent rows and fights. This is because this will be your biggest weapon against the social worker. You need to be able to squarely face the reality and possibility of separation from your partner, and when you have done this, you will have the freedom to explore other less drastic measures.

Have no doubt about this: where domestic violence occurs (especially where it gets physical) in the presence or vicinity of a child under ten, one of the adult parties almost always gets arrested. And where an arrest is made, there will be bail conditions preventing contact for a set period of time. The other parent left to care for the child is now under assessment to ascertain their capacity to protect the child. It is in this assessment that a lot of parents make the mistakes that lead to the child being removed from the home.

Common mistakes the other parent very often makes include; *Defending the perpetrator parent and minimising the incident and Local Authority concerns*

Insisting they cannot be without the perpetrator (for any reason) and that they will reunite with them.

Enabling the perpetrator to breach bail conditions by encouraging contact with the family unit.

Keeping to bail conditions but resuming the relationship after the bail conditions expire without informing the social worker.

Assuring the social worker, they will keep to a plan of separation, but sneak the perpetrator parent in when no one is looking.

Doing the point above and asking the children to lie when asked about this.

These points above continue to rear their head among parents who are dealing with social services for the first time. They appear so obvious that these parents never stop to think that other parents have already thought about and tried these approaches. They certainly never stop to think that the social worker and other professionals would also be familiar with these approaches. After reading this book, you now know that the best approaches to take in the case of intervention for domestic violence are ones that run directly counter to the above.

Advisable approaches to take in interventions for domestic violence

Accept and be prepared to make a clean and permanent break from the perpetrator if all other courses of action fail.

Acknowledge in full the severity of the incident and the concerns of the social worker.

Accept responsibility for your role in the DV incident.

Be honest about the value of the relationship for you and how much you want to salvage it, but express commitment to working with the social worker and the care plan.

Never encourage a breach of bail conditions–at least not with physical or in-person contact with the child/children.

Never lead the perpetrator to believe you would ever prosecute a relationship with them sneakily, not in any of your communications, especially written ones, in case these are submitted against you.

Be open and honest with the social worker about all plans to resume the relationship.

Along with doing the point above, you and the perpetrator must commit to engaging with rehabilitation courses suggested by the social worker.

However, in reference to the last two points, always adhere to the immediate separation rules put in place by the social worker following the DV incident. After that, you can discuss with them and draw up a plan for your reunion with your partner, as the social worker will deem it safe and manageable.

Never let the perpetrator come in contact with the children against the social worker's advice or the care plan.

Never ask or require the children to lie on your and/or the perpetrator's behalf.

Finally, in the case where you are willing to end the relationship, do not delay in taking out a non-molestation order against the perpetrator.

All of the above approaches or some in combination will win the trust of the social worker and other professionals and help reduce the level of intervention or knock it out entirely.

DEALING WITH INTERVENTION DUE TO SUBSTANCE MISUSE

Unsurprisingly, substance misuse is the most damaging and problematic of the Toxic Trio that a family can face. There is a lot already out there on the dangers of substance misuse and the hold it can have over parents, rendering them incapable of making care decisions or taking care actions consistently. It can also make them emotionally absent from their children. I will not do a rehash of the very public knowledge about drug addiction and how it can take control of a person. I will point out, however, that very often, substance misuse is either a main driver for any of the other two of the trio or a recourse due to the other two, so that where there is poor mental health, for instance, it could have been driven by substance misuse or pushed the parent to substance misuse. The same applies to domestic violence.

However, of the three, substance misuse is, ironically, the most commonly well-managed in respect of caring for children. There are more children living safely and happily in households with substance misuse issues under a well-monitored care plan than can be said for any of the other two difficulties, taken in isolation. This is because substance misuse has a very wide range in terms of its applicability, and there is such a wide variety of what can be termed 'substances', both legal and illegal. There is, after all, a sizeable number of adults who are addicted to prescription drugs.

Therefore, the first aim of the social worker when they visit you is to try to ascertain just how entrenched your level of addiction or dependence is and what functionality you can retain when using the substance or when not. With this information, they will aim to put together a safety plan to manage your drug use in a way that allows you to care for the children. They will seek to do this with the support of your family/friends' network, safely.

I have worked with so many families where substance misuse is an issue, and even when we are in care proceedings, I see a repeat of the same mistakes that many parents make. They lie about their substance use. This is not a helpful approach to take with the social worker in any way because social services are evidence-driven. As I have already outlined above, a social work assessment or intervention would not easily be triggered without a good evidence base that shows reasonable cause. So, when you, as a parent, lie to the social worker, they will not take your word for it. And if the social worker is not convinced, then their concern for the child/children not only remains but escalates–because they can find no way to address the concern with you not being honest.

Of course, you do not admit to something that is not true if that applies, because in that case, the truth of the issue will be tested in the intervention escalation process.

In most cases, parents lying about their drug use happens when they are on the cusp of care proceedings because the evidence that the Local Authority employs to get into proceedings is usually stark. However, there are cases where the parent is known to have a history of drug use. When the opportunity arises for them to be assessed as safe to care for a child, and they are, naturally, questioned about their current drug use, they think it most appropriate to lie.

It would be pretty unusual, maybe rare, for social services to entrust a child into the care of a parent with a history of drug use without a comprehensive drug test, and in the court process, a drug test is also employed for evidence. So, the point is this–lying is only ever going to backfire. When the test confirms that you are lying, all hope of being able to work with you to put together a safety plan to manage your drug use is dashed. You are branded as dishonest, uncooperative, not unwilling to work with professionals to put together a safety plan, and therefore, there is very little chance you can care for the child/ren safely.

On the other hand, these are the steps to take when dealing with intervention due to substance misuse;

- Accept and be honest about your drug use–what drug/s and the level of your drug use.
- Be ahead of the intervention and contact drug and addiction agencies, and start work with them.
- Acknowledge in full the severity of the concerns of the Local Authority to the social worker.
- Be honest about what you can cope with in giving up that drug; do not promise something you cannot achieve, or you risk being seen as not being genuine in your engagement with professionals.
- Always have your family/friends network primed and ready to support you in putting together a care plan with the social worker. This may include someone who can provide temporary care for the children while you go through the intervention.
- Finally, keep engaging with your addiction support worker at all times.

Consider these two scenarios: Mother is a heroin user and has clearly exposed the children in her care to this drug as well as to the associated dangers that come with it. A man who should not be around children is found in her home using heroin with her. The children are removed under police protection and taken to a family member. During the intervention, the mother is honest about her addiction and her difficulties. She is willing to work with agencies to undergo rehabilitation, but she makes it clear to the social worker that she will not find it easy and can only take so much. A care plan is put together that involves the family network, and with the advice of the addiction support worker, this plan looks at the mother's drug use and rehab work and how she can safely care for the children with this ongoing. Contact is phased in to match the information gathered, and at the end of 6 months, the children are back living with their mother, who is still working to keep her drug habit at bay.

On the other hand, the father is very functional and can care for the children safely. In fact, he has had care of them for a three-month period on his own with no trouble at all. However, they are now in proceedings due to the children being removed from the mother's care. Father has P.R. and rightly requests to care for his children and is favoured by all parties in court to have the children, but because the case is already in court and there had been some concerns raised about his own drug use, a drug test is ordered. However, Dad has told the court and the social worker that he does not use drugs in any way at all. In fact, this goes against his morals, and he would never think of touching any drugs. After months of holding this position, the drug test reveals months of cocaine use. Father continues to deny any drug use, claiming the test must have been faulty and giving reasons to back this up. Other, less comprehensive drugs test was commissioned to give him a chance to prove his claims, but he avoids these with more excuses. The social worker concludes in his assessment that since the father has not been honest about his drug use, it cannot be ascertained how much he uses, the context in which he uses these, or the frequency, and because of his dishonesty, a safety plan could not be put in place. The children are placed in long-term care.

From the above two examples, it is clear that the mother who was, on paper, the higher risk of the two, was ascertained as safer to care as she gave the most opportunity for a safety plan to be drawn up. As a result of his dishonesty, on the other hand, the father, who was so close to getting the children back into his care, loses them to the care system.

DEALING WITH INTERVENTION DUE TO PHYSICAL DISCIPLINE/CHASTISEMENT

This is an area of intervention that is becoming more and more common with the growth in immigration. We find that a lot of the cases where this issue is found fall within immigrant families, and we also find these cases with ethnic minority groups.

For many non-British cultures, sparing the rod is equivalent to 'spoiling the child'. However, in England, using physical discipline on children is a social care concern that could also result in criminal prosecution depending on the circumstances and the discretion of the police.

Very often, this issue comes to the attention of social services from children reporting about their home life at school or to some other professional. Where a professional passes on this information to the social care safeguarding department, it will almost always lead to a threshold discussion between social care and the police to decide if a section 47 investigation is needed. Also, very often, the outcome of this discussion will be that a section 47 investigation is indeed needed; what will vary is the decision whether the police needs to be involved, to investigate a potential criminal offence or not, and whether it should be a single or joint investigation.

Now, it is at the discretion of the police how they address reports of physical discipline, so the guidelines are not clear-cut. However, there are certain things that may guide their decision to get involved: one–if there are any marks, bruises or injuries on the child; two–if the report shows the punishments are calculated, planned out and, therefore, regarded as being of a sinister nature; three–if the report shows the punishments are of themselves harsh, cruel and/or barbaric. This third point, which is subjective, ties in with the second point.

Therefore, a lot of African families who employ physical discipline as a standard way to raise children will fall victim to the second and third points. This is because they, necessarily, would have evolved a calculated and planned-out way to mete out these punishments. Therefore, the punishments will almost always come across as sinister and cruel.

On the other hand, lashing out in the heat of the moment is rarely seen as sinister or worthy of being investigated as a crime; more often than not, it is seen as simply a social care issue. Of course, if this becomes a recurring thing, that will lead to an escalation in how social care and the police manage this.

Let's look at these two examples: *A child of ten discloses at school that she is scared to go home. She says she is often hit at home by her father, who is African, and her mum, who is white British, does nothing to stop him. Father will often tell them to lie down and hit them on the bottom with an implement. Sometimes, she will ask them to hold out their palms and hit them there. The punishments are always planned and calculated.*

A threshold discussion was held, and although all other measures of care for this child and her siblings were great, the police were worried about the seemingly sinister and calculated approach to the discipline. Professionals agreed that there should be a joint section 47 investigation between the police and social care. Although there were no bruises or marks on the child, the police spoke to the child's siblings, who corroborated her story. On this information, both parents were arrested, and the children had to go stay with their maternal aunt. The parents were released on bail with conditions not to have contact with the children unless as stipulated by social services. The case went to the Child Protection Conference, and the children were placed on a Child Protection Plan. It took another four months before they were able to return home.

On the other hand....*A child of five had disclosed at school that her mother had struck her hard on the thigh, causing bruising. Pictures of this bruise were taken by teachers and sent to social care. A threshold discussion was convened, and the situation was detailed further; Mum had been very stressed with the child not getting ready for school. The child had refused to put her socks on, and her mother had lashed out, striking her. All other measures of care for the child were fine. The decision of professionals was that it should be a single agency, a section 47 investigation by social care. The police did not think they had a role to play; Mum needed more support with managing the child's behaviours. The section 47 investigation did not lead to a referral to a Child Protection Conference either, but was closed with support recommended.*

Now, if you, as a parent, get a call from social services (and/or the police) relating to your use of physical discipline on your child, you need to first be aware that defending your 'right' to hit your child is not a wise move. You have no such rights–not in England. On the contrary, the child has a right to be safe from any harmful or distressing physical contact. If you take this stance, you are only confirming to professionals that you are not a safe parent for the child, and the child will continue to be at risk of harm in your care. This could lead to drastic measures such as separation between you and the child.

On the other hand, you should listen to the concerns of the social worker and/or the police and admit to your actions and not only resolve to not do so again but also ask for support with alternative means to parent safely. You may be asked to sign an agreement with social care that you will desist from that point on from all forms of physical discipline; you should adhere to the terms of that agreement. You may also be required to attend parenting courses on how to better and safely parent. Again, you should work with the social worker on this.

If the police were to get involved, there is a very good chance that you would be arrested, and the children would need to be cared for by someone else for some time, as you would end up under bail conditions that restrict your contact with your child. However, again, this is not a clear-cut cut, and the outcome of the police visiting your home could vary depending on how you present and address the concerns.

The good news, however, is that physical discipline is a social care and criminal concern that is rarely treated on its own when the safety of the child is being considered. It is not a foundational ill like the toxic trio that undermines the capacity of the parent to actually care. It is often simply a style of parenting (erroneous as it is) that parents employ. So, social care professionals and the police will also be considering other areas of the child's life, like their home, school attendance, presentation in school, social, emotional, and cognitive development–markers of how the child is actually being looked after by their parents. If these areas are good, then the case will likely end up as a social care area, and support to be given to the parents. Even where the police get involved, it is unlikely that it will end in prosecution.

If, on the other hand, there is a catalogue of concerns in other areas and it is clear that the parenting of the children is faulty in many respects, then not only would the social care and police intervention be more serious, but it would also lead to more stringent separation measures.

Depending on how the interaction between you and the professionals goes, the section 47 investigation may conclude with no further action, or it may lead to a Child Protection Conference. If you are arrested by the police, then it will almost certainly go to a Child Protection Conference. See the chapter on Child Protection Conference.

CHILD IN NEED PLANNING

Now, most of the time that a social worker will come out to 'have a chat' with parents and carry out an assessment of the child's situation, it will end up with a 'No Further Action' outcome. This is because a lot of the time, all they will need to do is draw up a safety plan with you, the parent, to address the issues or difficulties they uncover in the assessment. And that safety plan will be sufficient to address the problems, and there will be no further need for social services intervention.

Of course, as already outlined above, if the parent fails to work honestly and committedly to the social worker, what could have been sorted neatly as a more minor matter could escalate into something more serious than it needs to be.

At other times, the social worker will find that the safety plan itself may not be sufficient and that there would need to be some more work by other professionals at a lower level to support the parents and child. At this point, the social worker may 'step the case down' to Early Help or to a family support practitioner. This practitioner will work with the family in strengthening their relationship at this lower level.

However, a small percentage of the cases that social workers assess will end up on a Child in Need plan. This is when the social worker identifies a more complex mix of issues that would require a multi-agency approach; there would need to be a CIN plan drawn up in this case, with all the agencies drafted in to do their bit of work with the child. The social worker would convene a CIN meeting every 6 weeks where all these agencies and parents come together to review how things are progressing for the family.

Now, a child being stepped up to CIN could also be an indication that you, the parent, had failed to proactively engage either with practitioners at the social work assessment stage or at the Early Help stage. Considering that the concerns for the child would persist, social services would rightly be worried that the child continues not to have their needs met, and parents are not engaging. Therefore, they take the child to CIN so they can more directly monitor parents' input.

Now, *Under a CIN plan, parents have P.R. and do not have to engage with the social worker or professionals, but do be careful. In your case, the CIN plan may have been put in place to evidence your participation or lack of, so that when the case gets escalated, there is evidence to show if your parenting capacity is good enough or not.*

If you are going to not participate in CIN planning for your child, be sure that it is a situation where the case has been stepped down from a more advanced risk management stage to the CIN stage; for instance, the case was previously in court with the child under a Care Order or the child was previously under a Child Protection Plan and now the child has been stepped down to a CIN plan. This would mean that the main issues would have already been resolved, and the Local Authority would not have strong enough evidence to escalate upwards again.

PARENTAL CONSENT

Whilst under CIN planning, the social worker will visit your home to see the child every four weeks; they will have forewarned you of the visit. Now, depending on the concerns, the social worker may want to speak to the child alone. They will need your consent for this to happen. At this stage, nothing happens to the child without your consent. The social worker may have concerns that you may pose a risk of harm to the child at some level, and is looking to speak to the child to evidence this. Depending on what the child says, it may mean more CIN planning or an escalation. However, you can refuse consent for this to happen, and the social worker has no right either to go and speak to the child in school without your consent. You may want to head this off by advising the school to get confirmation of your consent before allowing the social worker to speak to your child.

Just like with the police, in social services intervention, what is rarely mentioned is that you do have the right not to incriminate yourself. This sounds bad when we consider that it is a child's welfare in the balance; however, rights and principles exist for a reason–to ward off abuse of power and position and unjust practice. If the concern in question is strong enough, there would be other evidence for it; after all, the concern had come to light in the first place from some source. Basically, the social worker will need to find the evidence for their concerns themselves without your help. You have the right not to facilitate something that would not be in your favour.

Just like with the police and the age-old advice not to speak to the police, under arrest, without a lawyer present, it may be advisable that you do not consent for your child to speak to the social worker when a suspected risk of harm, with no evidence base, is being investigated against you. Let the authorities find the evidence for themselves; this way, if there is evidence and it is significant enough, it will be found. If not, you will be spared the stress of a probably pointless investigation. Of course, like with a police investigation, if evidence of harm to the child was eventually found, your earlier reluctance to give consent and/or reticence could harm your defence.

Let's look at this example: *A report has come in from a random woman on the bus; she had seen a five-year-old child who was being naughty on the bus to school, and his grandmother had smacked him twice. The report also claims that Gran was being severe with him and one time dragged him roughly when he was moving away from her. The child lives with Gran and dad; Gran brings him into school as dad goes to work early in the morning.*

The social care first response team cannot do much with this information without speaking to the child first, as it is third-party information. They call you Dad at work and tell you about the report. They request your consent to go and speak to the child at school. It is well within your rights to refuse the request. Of course, if you were complicit in any abuse of the child, you would probably not give consent anyway, but if you wanted your child to be safe, you would plan to address this yourself with your mother when you got back home. Furthermore, the child is seen by professionals in school every day, and they talk to the child about home life, and any such concerns will come to the fore at some point. The social care team would more likely, actually, request school as a first resort to tease information from the child about his experience on the bus and being parented. This way, this concern will ultimately be evidenced if it is true and/or significant enough.

If someone at school speaks to your child about the smacking and he confirms it, the social care team will hold a threshold discussion with the police to conduct a section 47 investigation (described earlier, and more on this later). If a s47 investigation is agreed, this would give the team the right to speak to the child without your consent. Until that happens, you are not required to help them out.

The whole point of the parents' stance in the above example is to limit any unnecessary intrusions into a family's life and abuse of power by the social worker. Children are, very often, in the eyes of professionals outside the family, be it the midwife, health visitor, GP, nursery and school staff, etc. It is these professionals who will be the source of evidence for the Local Authority when the social worker does not have consent for direct access to the child.

If, however, there was no other avenue for professionals to have eyes on the child, say, the child was being home-schooled, then it would be imperative that you, the parent, allow access to the child, as there would be no other way for professionals to ascertain that the child was safe. Of course, it would be within your rights as a parent to refuse. The Local Authority would then consider seeking legal authority from the Court to gain access to the child; this may be via an application for an Assessment Order or other means.

The downside of you refusing access to the child in a situation like this is that if the assessment eventually went ahead and it was identified that the child was indeed suffering physical abuse (or any other harm) at any level, then your initial reluctance would be interpreted as of sinister intent and the concern taken much more seriously than ordinarily.

If at some point, this child comes under a CIN plan for this concern of physical abuse, this will likely be alongside other difficulties at home. This is a good example of when not to refuse to engage with the CIN planning as a parent. If you do, you will be inviting an escalation of processes into what is called Child Protection Planning.

CHILD PROTECTION PLANNING

Child protection planning is the first of the two advanced stages of risk management before care proceedings are initiated. Usually, the trigger for child protection planning is when a child is suspected to be at risk of or already suffering significant harm in the care of their parents or family. When this happens, the social care team, along with the police, would hold what is called a Threshold Discussion to ascertain if the situation merits an investigation into the risk of significant harm to a child. This investigation is more commonly referred to as a section 47 investigation.

Now, when you hear a social worker say that they are undertaking a s47 investigation, be aware that not only are the concerns being treated as serious, but that at that point, your consent can be dispensed with to speak to the child or have access to the child.

There are two types of s47 investigation–single and joint. A single investigation simply means that the police have already judged that there is no reason to suspect a crime had been committed and, therefore, the investigation is one for social care alone. Following this, a joint is the opposite; it is an investigation jointly undertaken between the police and social care.

Keep in mind that if you, as a parent, are the subject of a joint investigation, it is highly likely that this will end up in Child Protection. There are some factors that determine this. The child should be judged as currently at risk of significant harm, so even if the child was in the care of another family member, since the suspect parent has P.R. and direct right of access to the child, the child will be judged as being at risk of significant harm. If, however, the child was in the care of the other parent who also had P.R., then they would not be judged to be at this risk (as the parent's P.R. would match up against that of the suspect parent), and therefore a s47 investigation would not be necessary, even though police action might still continue. Remember, a s47 investigation is a social care process; its absence does not mean the police would not still act against a suspect parent unilaterally to address a crime.

Let's look at two examples to make this clearer; *So, we have mum who is basically an alcoholic, and there have been several interventions in the past to support her with her alcohol use under CIN planning. The last time, she worked really well with agencies and was judged to be doing quite well with managing her alcohol use and meeting the child's needs.*

A few months later, after a few reports from school staff concerned that she may be drinking again, she was arrested for drink driving with the child in the car. The police removed the child from her care under Police Protection and, having discovered there was a dad with P.R., called him up and placed the child with him.

Following the process, social care would hold a Threshold Discussion with the police, and following the process, this would not meet the threshold for a s47 investigation unless there were any concerns about Dad's capacity to protect. As at the time the Threshold Discussion was held, the child was no longer at risk of significant harm and was in the care of someone who also had P.R.

The police may also put bail conditions on the mother not to have contact with the child within a certain timeframe within which social services could support the dad to apply for prohibitive orders from the court, against mum, to protect the child.

If the police felt there were more actions they needed to carry out in respect of the incident, this would be a police matter that social care could contribute to, but not as part of a s47 investigation.

This case would certainly, therefore, not go on to Child Protection Planning.

In contrast, *we have the same situation as above, except this time the child's dad was absent or cannot be located. The child is placed with the maternal aunt instead. This case would meet the threshold for a single or joint investigation, depending on whether the police felt there was more work they needed to do. At the time the Threshold Discussion was held, the child was not ordinarily safe from access to his mother as he was living with someone who did not have P.R. And, considering the history of mum's alcohol use and past interventions, it would almost certainly end up in Child Protection Planning.*

Most cases that come into Child Protection, however, graduate from Child in Need planning. This happens where there is very little improvement in the child's welfare, wellbeing, or circumstances despite the support being offered to the parent. Usually, this is because the parent is either not fully committed to working with professionals or to implementing the recommendations of professionals. This is why, as I explained in the last chapter, a refusal to work with professionals under CIN should be justified by either there being a single issue that you are confident you can fix without intervention or that the case has actually stepped down from a more advanced stage to CIN and, therefore, is at its safest point. Otherwise, you could be providing the required evidence for Child Protection Planning.

Know this: *Social Care processes, in practice, are not as linear as I have laid them out. Human situations are complex, so depending on the case, two or more stages of risk management could be activated almost at the same time. A child could come into care from first contact with social services, depending on the context, and another child could spend years of their life in intervention, but always living with their parents. It is important you catch up to what stage of intervention you are in, from either what the social worker is telling you or what their report/s says. With that knowledge, use the tips in this book to respond accordingly.*

From when a child comes under a Child Protection Plan, be assured that, as much as the social worker will continue trying to support you to keep to the plan, they are also gathering evidence of the contrary in preparation for possible future proceedings. Under CP, you, as the parent, have little room to drop the ball. This is the time to begin to show by your actions that you can follow the CP plan and keep the child safe. However, like I pointed out earlier, if you have any difficulties with this, you should be honest about it. There is a forum in place where you can do this, and it is called the Child Protection Conference.

Child Protection Conference

A child can only be judged as being under a CP plan if or when this has been agreed at a CP conference. After a s47 investigation is completed and the social worker and their management team are satisfied that this child is indeed at risk of significant harm, they would request that the case be sent to an Initial CP conference. There would be a social work assessment completed that explores the risk of significant harm that social care is concerned about in more depth. This report would also have a safety plan drawn up, which would be the plan going over to the conference. It is at the conference that this plan would be either approved, amended, or even rejected–as a CP plan.

You, as a parent, would be invited to the conference; you can bring with you someone to support you, or you can request that an advocate be provided for you.

It is at the conference that the concerns for the child would be discussed among professionals in depth, and it may well indeed turn out that the concerns upon examination fizzle out to nothing (although this is incredibly rare). However, this is where you can talk about your situation and how it affects your parenting, which could not be easily captured in an assessment. This is also where you talk about your limitation; I have observed parents speak honestly about how much they can commit to in reducing their substance or alcohol intake within a given timeframe. I have also witnessed honest admission from parents about their emotional regulation and what they would react strongly to from their children. And the resulting CP plan had taken account of these admissions in building a plan tailored to help them succeed. Following all discussions, the professionals attending the meeting would be asked at the end to give their views on whether the child should be under a CP plan or not. They could vote yes or no; almost all of the time, professionals would vote yes because there is usually good evidence provided before a case is even accepted as meriting being brought to a CP conference.

The CP plan that is approved at this initial conference would be reviewed every 6 weeks in a minor meeting similar to the conference, but chaired by the social worker. This is called a Core Group meeting. This review will monitor the progress of the plan and evidence parents' participation in this. This carries on until the next conference, which is called a Review Child Protection Conference, and where the CP plan in its most up-to-date state is once again reviewed. It is at an RCPC that big changes to the plan are made, including a decision to step the plan down from Child Protection back to Child in Need. This only happens when it is evident that parents are working with professionals to keep to the plan, and the risks to the children have significantly reduced.

As a parent, you want to get to that point where the case is stepped down from CP to CIN; to facilitate this, you do the same things as already advised in this book.

You must work and make it obvious you are working with professionals to keep to the CP plan.

You should attend the Core Group meetings and make the children accessible for visits.

If there are difficulties that you are struggling with that triggered the case going to CP, whether from DV, Mental Health, Substance Misuse, or any other issue, you should take proactive steps to seek support from agencies and stick to the plan of support.

If, on the other hand, the concerns persist or get worse, or if you, the parent, continue not to follow the CP plan, then the Local Authority would escalate the process to the Public Law Outline process.

PUBLIC LAW OUTLINE

The Public Law Outline–commonly called PLO–process is the last gasp attempt by the Local Authority to avoid initiating proceedings and to give parents a chance to pull things back from what is now the brink. It is a peace conference convened to prevent a battle in court, which could be stressful for the child and family. To kickstart the process, you, as a parent, would be invited to a PLO meeting by the social care management team.

The PLO meeting is the first and introductory step to the PLO process; it is where the stage for what happens in the process is set. This meeting is legally witnessed, and the letter you would receive as a parent would give you advice on where and how to get legal representation. You are supposed to attend this meeting with your solicitors, and the Local Authority will have theirs at the meeting as well.

When you are invited to the PLO meeting, you should understand that, at this point, you are very close to care proceedings and your room for negotiation is now quite limited. The meeting itself spells this out. It is not a meeting where much back-and-forth discussion is ordinarily allowed or excuses/reasons are entertained. The Local Authority would be interested in only one thing–making sure your solicitor is present to witness the tasks and plan they are requesting of you, and that your failure to adhere to them would most certainly lead to the issuing of proceedings.

Usually, the meeting starts with the Local Authority narrating the background that had led to the process being instigated, the concerns of the Local Authority, and then moves from there to the tasks they expect to see completed. These tasks would vary depending on the concerns in question but would typically include parenting assessments, courses or programmes to address a particular issue, scientific testing to evidence a concern, or evidence of progressive work with a support agency on a particular issue.

Your solicitors would be there to help you clarify any confusion, raise any worries or limitations you may have, and also advise you on how to work around these. This meeting does not usually take a long time, as it is supposed to be a one-way street. You probably do not need much advice to understand that at this stage, you would have missed ample opportunities to limit the level of social services intervention in your family life. You certainly do not need to be told that the only way forward at this point is to complete all the tasks instructed by the Local Authority and to keep to the care plan. Any deviation at this point would lead to care proceedings being initiated.

The PLO process is higher placed than Child Protection, although both could be running side by side; Child Protection planning is only terminated early when care proceedings are initiated.

CARE PROCEEDINGS AND INTERIM CARE ORDER

You will know when care proceedings are initiated against you for the purpose of seeking a care order over your child. You will be informed by a formal letter from the Local Authority's legal team. You will also be advised on how to get yourself legal representation, and there will be some advice on seeking legal aid. Often, this last advice will not be needed by you, as you would have already gone through that process for the Public Law Outline.

At this stage, you will be facing the Local Authority's application that the Court grant it an Interim Care Order over your child whilst further assessments are undertaken to determine your capacity to safely care for the child. This application marks the start of care proceedings, which in principle are supposed to run for a maximum of 26 weeks; however, this is often not the case as this timescale is often exceeded. The idea is that there should be no delay for the child and that their permanent care plan should be decided within a reasonable timeframe.

When the application becomes active, the Court appoints a Guardian to represent the interests of the child; the Guardian, in turn, instructs an advocate to represent the child as a separate party in court. The Guardian is also a social worker who works in an advisory role to the court. The Guardian will at some point come out to speak with you and the carers (at the time) of the child in order to get a good understanding of the situation. The role of the Guardian is to scrutinise the work of the Local Authority and ensure that what they are proposing and their work is indeed in the child's best interest. So, at this stage, when you have been drawn into care proceedings, the best person to get on side would be the Guardian.

At this early phase, the Guardian is a newcomer and has no direct knowledge of you, the parent, your family, or the child, except for what has been written in reports. Therefore, you have another opportunity to make a first impression with the Guardian. Of course, you would be making a mistake to try to make out to the Guardian that the reports by the Local Authority are wrong or that you are blameless. This is usually a warning sign to any childcare professional that a parent is not ready or able to accept responsibility for past failings, acknowledge concerns, and, therefore, may not be able to attend to these concerns.

Know this; It is always a wise move to be accepting of your role in the dysfunctionality that has occurred, to take responsibility for your actions, and acknowledge the harm the child would have been exposed to. This portrays you in the eyes of professionals at any stage of intervention, even in care proceedings, as probably able to take the next step towards change.

And remember; The Guardian is your friend!

After being honest about your role in the whole situation to the Guardian, then commit to working to evidence change or a capacity for change. You do this in how committedly you attend meetings with the social worker, multi-agency meetings (Child in Care Review Meetings), and meetings with other professionals in respect of the child. The more of a friend you can get the Guardian to be to you, the more the Care Proceedings will tilt in your favour. The Guardian is known to have great influence with the Court.

Before the above paragraph takes effect, the child would have been placed under an ICO; the evidence that the Local Authority presents at the initial hearing for an ICO is usually formidable enough for the Court to grant the ICO that the Local Authority requests.

This is a reasonable step as the ICO is only to ensure the child is safe in the care of the Local Authority whilst further assessment of the parents is undertaken to determine what orders will be made at the Final Hearing. This period of Care

Proceedings, therefore, represents the final opportunity for you, the parent, to make or show a capacity for change that the Court (all the parties) can be confident in enough to discharge the ICO and return the child to your care.

If you cannot show this capacity for change at the very least, the Final Hearing will see orders being made that 'permanently' separate the child from your care. Depending on the age of the child, this could be under a Care Order to remain in foster care or under Care and Placement Orders (for very young children under 5), which are the pre-requisite orders to seek an adoptive home for the child.

You do not want to ever come this far.

CHILD IN CARE

Your child is classed as a child in care when they are legally under the care of the Local Authority, underlined by a legal order. Most of these orders are granted at Court, either as an Interim Care Order or a Care Order; however, the Section 20 order is simply activated through the consent of parents for the Local Authority to care for their child. A young person over the age of 16 can also consent for the Local Authority to take charge of their care.

An Interim Care Order is granted during care proceedings and, as already described above, gives room for further assessments of the parents or family to care for the child. However, by the end of the proceedings, if the evaluations of parents are negative, then often a Care Order is granted, for the child to be cared for by the Local Authority for the remainder of their childhood. Now, there is a healthy percentage of care proceedings where the final outcome is Care and Placement Orders; this is basically the setup for the child to be sought by adoptive parents. This book does not cover that scenario.

If your child, however, has become subject to a Care Order, then your work as a parent is not done, although it may well seem that way. No, the Care Process is always and should always be open to the prospect of reunification with family. In fact, the

Child in Care Review Meetings that happen usually every six months are generally about reviewing the prospect of reunification, whilst looking at how the child's care is being provided by the Local Authority.

Therefore, although it will be a crushing blow 'losing' your child to the 'system', the best way forward after proceedings are concluded, is to address the concerns that led to the child being removed and continue working with the social care team on your child's care planning. For many parents, getting support from partner agencies set up to provide aftercare to parents suffering from the trauma of losing their child to the care system is a good first step.

There have been a lot of parents in my experience who have moved on quickly after the proceedings, to begin to attend to every concern of the Local Authority, about their capacity to parent. They have sought therapy, rehabilitation, support from relevant agencies, gone on courses, got support and treatment for their mental health, and so on. However, crucially, whilst putting their lives back together, they had remained very much in touch and connected with the social care team on care planning for their child. They had continued to religiously attend family time with the child; they had been present at every Child in Care Review Meeting, attended Personal Education Plan meetings or requested reports from these, and had generally remained an active voice and presence in the child's care journey.

And in the end, for all these parents, there had come a point when the Child in Care Review had assessed the changes they had made in their lives and their proactiveness in attending to the child's care planning and welfare. As a result, the CIC Review had recommended that a reunification screening and further parenting capacity assessment be completed following the screening being positive. For most of these cases, the assessment had ended up being positive, and the child, with careful planning, had been transitioned back home to their family.

Of course, this is never that straightforward. There will be situations where the child's care with their Local Authority carers or maybe even kinship carers is so settled that it is assessed that it would not be in their best interest to move them, despite the changes parents have made.

All the same-know this; As already stated in this book, the main aim of the Local Authority is to keep children with their families. This aim remains alive and in focus through the various stages of intervention and even when the child is removed from your care. It is important not to lose sight of this fact. As long as you, the parent, can attend to your difficulties and to the concerns of the Local Authority, the likelihood is that your child will be reunited with your family.

CONCLUSION

We have been through the basics and a few advanced processes of the Local Authority as they work with families via social services intervention.

You will have seen that opening yourself up to honest, collaborative working with the social worker, knowing your rights and the limits of what the social worker can legally do, and in the latter stages, befriending the Guardian will improve your chances significantly in having a less complicated and smoother journey through any intervention.

One thing you will need to understand is that the first aim of the Local Authority, as dictated by legislation, is to keep children in their families. The social worker's first aim is to try to support parents to care for their children safely.

Once you understand this, you will see that from the outset, the intervention is usually yours to make worse, yours to complicate–not the social workers.

You should now have a better understanding of the job of the social worker, their role, remit, and limitations. This will help you tailor your expectations of them more realistically.

I hope that with what you have learned in this book, you can support yourself or someone you know through what is often perceived and experienced as a stressful journey through social services intervention.

www.ingramcontent.com/pod-product-compliance
Ingram Content Group UK Ltd.
Pitfield, Milton Keynes, MK11 3LW, UK
UKHW021240300926
15471UKWH00014B/901

9 798232 001551